INTO Wild Galápagos

BLACKBIRCH®
PRESS

THOMSON
————✳————
GALE

San Diego • Detroit • New York • San Francisco • Cleveland • New Haven, Conn. • Waterville, Maine • London • Munich

LIBRARY OF CONGRESS CATALOGING-IN-PUBLICATION DATA

Into Wild Galápagos / Elaine Pascoe, book editor.
    p. cm. — (The Jeff Corwin experience)
Based on an episode from a Discovery Channel program hosted by Jeff Corwin.
Summary: Television personality Jeff Corwin takes the reader on an expedition to the Galápagos Islands, home to some of the world's most unique wildlife, including iguanas, giant tortoises, and tropical penguins.
Includes bibliographical references and index.
  ISBN 1-56711-857-7 (hardback : alk. paper) — ISBN 1-4103-0173-7 (pbk. : alk. paper)
  1. Zoology—Galápagos Islands—Juvenile literature. [1. Zoology—Galápagos Islands. 2. Galápagos Islands—Description and travel. 3. Corwin, Jeff.] I. Pascoe, Elaine. II. Corwin, Jeff. III. Series.

  QL345.G2I58 2004
  591.9866'5—dc21

2003009280

Printed in China
10 9 8 7 6 5 4 3 2 1

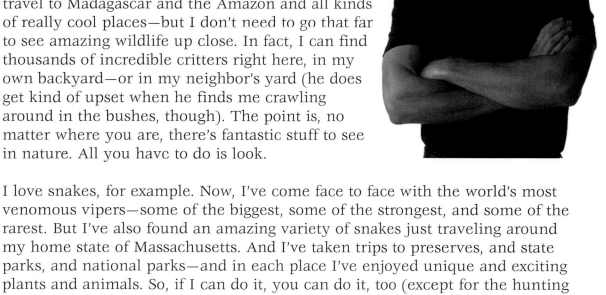

Ever since I was a kid, I dreamed about traveling around the world, visiting exotic places, and seeing all kinds of incredible animals. And now, guess what? That's exactly what I get to do!

Yes, I am incredibly lucky. But, you don't have to have your own television show on Animal Planet to go off and explore the natural world around you. I mean, I travel to Madagascar and the Amazon and all kinds of really cool places—but I don't need to go that far to see amazing wildlife up close. In fact, I can find thousands of incredible critters right here, in my own backyard—or in my neighbor's yard (he does get kind of upset when he finds me crawling around in the bushes, though). The point is, no matter where you are, there's fantastic stuff to see in nature. All you have to do is look.

I love snakes, for example. Now, I've come face to face with the world's most venomous vipers—some of the biggest, some of the strongest, and some of the rarest. But I've also found an amazing variety of snakes just traveling around my home state of Massachusetts. And I've taken trips to preserves, and state parks, and national parks—and in each place I've enjoyed unique and exciting plants and animals. So, if I can do it, you can do it, too (except for the hunting venomous snakes part!). So, plan a nature hike with some friends. Organize some projects with your science teacher at school. Ask mom and dad to put a state or a national park on the list of things to do on your next family vacation. Build a bird house. Whatever. But get out there.

As you read through these pages and look at the photos, you'll probably see how jazzed I get when I come face to face with beautiful animals. That's good. I want you to feel that excitement. And I want you to remember that—even if you don't have your own TV show—you can still experience the awesome beauty of nature almost anywhere you go—any day of the week. I only hope that I can help bring that awesome power and beauty a little closer to you. Enjoy!

Best Wishes!

Jeff

INTO
Wild Galápagos

The amazing Galápagos Islands straddle the equator 600 miles off the coast of South America. Isolated from the mainland, with constant volcanic activity, they've become a living laboratory of evolution. Join me as we explore and encounter the strange and unique animals this place is famous for.

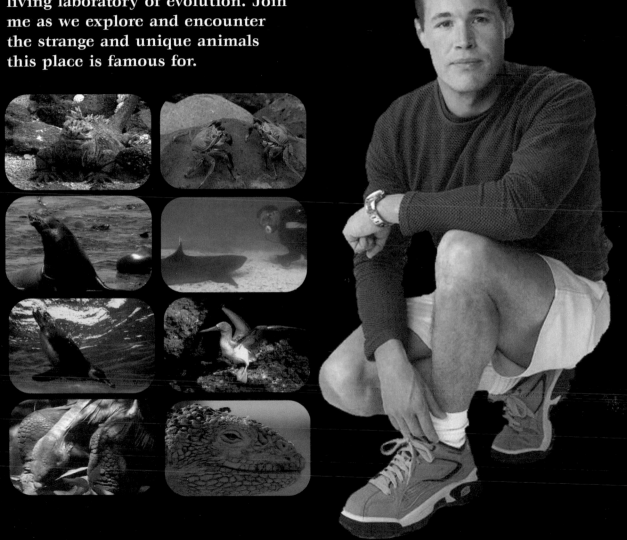

I'm Jeff Corwin.
Welcome to the Galápagos.

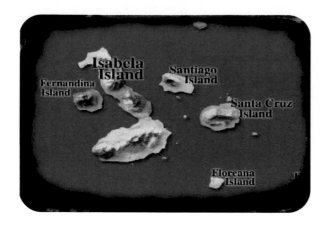

Galápagos is an incredible place.

Galápagos marine iguanas.

This is the Galápagos marine iguana, one of seven types of iguanas you'll find throughout these islands. They are extraordinary reptiles, hardy, and very fit for survival in this tough landscape.

The Galápagos Islands have a tough, volcanic landscape.

These iguanas are awesome.

That's Darwin up there. That's my ride down there.

We think of the Galápagos as a cornucopia filled with wildlife, but in fact these islands are species poor. That is, there are not a lot of different creatures living here. But what species are here are amazing— like these marine iguanas, they blow you away.

The famous nineteenth-century naturalist Charles Darwin used the Galápagos to illustrate his theories on the origin of species. Like Darwin, we'll travel by sailing ship through these islands. And we'll be seeing a ton of iguanas—even what researchers think may be an entirely new race of these unique reptiles.

Fernandina is the
youngest of the islands.

First stop, Fernandina, the youngest of these volcanic islands. This island is only seven hundred thousand years old. You can imagine it bubbling and pushing up from the oceans, steaming the water. In the end, it became a breeding ground for life. Just how did these animals get here?

The ancestor of the marine iguana drifted over from the mainland. It was your typical rain-forest iguana. Perhaps it drifted on a patch of vegetation. Maybe it was a female, ready to lay eggs. Or perhaps a small colony of iguanas made the trip on a drifting tree. Isolated in a habitat very different from the mainland of South America, these castaway iguanas evolved into very distinct species, marine species and land species.

These are the only lizards in the world that eat food from the ocean.

The marine iguanas are extraordinary because they survive in a saltwater environment. They come on land to lay their eggs and bask in the sun, but their food is saltwater algae, seaweed. They are the only lizards in the world that survive in a marine environment and harvest food from the sea, and they're found nowhere else but in the Galápagos.

When Darwin was here in 1835, he made a very interesting discovery about the marine iguanas. Today, you're not allowed to touch these animals. But Darwin did an experiment in which he hurled an iguana into the ocean and watched it swim back to land. He threw this creature back out in the water five or six times, and each time it swam back. He realized that—although the iguana was able to live in the ocean, like its distant ancestors—it felt safer on land.

These guys are medium sized and dark.

Each island has its own unique group of marine iguanas. On Isabela, they're huge. On Plaza Sur, they're tiny. And in some other islands, they're colorful. But here, on Fernandina, they're stocky, moderate in size, and very dark.

I call this one... "stocky."

That dark color has two important purposes. First, it's excellent camouflage. If you're living on a volcanic island and you're surrounded by black lava, what better way to blend in than to look like the lava?

Second, the dark color helps them stay warm. Fernandina is a little colder than some other parts of the Galápagos because upwellings of cold water surround the island. Like all reptiles, iguanas are cold-blooded and can't maintain a constant body temperature on their own. Dark coloring makes them like solar panels. They can suck heat energy from the sun, store it in their bodies, fire up their metabolisms, and then head on out to sea.

Cold water surrounds Fernandina.

Check this out—marine iguanas actually sneeze salt. They're not doing it to be rude. Living in a marine environment, they take in a lot of salt as they feed. And they get rid of it this way. Glands collect the salt from the bloodstream and then send it in flumes out of their nostrils.

It's true crustacean love...

Whoa—look at these crabs. They're a great example of how you can find the extraordinary in the middle of the ordinary. Sally Lightfoot crabs, a very common species of crustacean, litter these rocks. I've seen thousands of them, but this is the first time I've ever seen this. We actually have a pair of Sally Lightfoot crabs locked in an embrace. They're reproducing. The Galápagos, always filled with surprises.

Next, Plaza Sur, the Southern Plaza. No, it's not a tacky shopping mall.

Plaza Sur is one of the smallest islands, and it's home to a great colony of Galápagos sea lions, about fifty thousand of them. These animals are extraordinary swimmers. They can dive to hundreds of feet below the surface of the water to hunt for squid and other ocean animals.

These guys are incredible divers.

About fifty thousand sea lions live on Plaza Sur.

Happy bathers near the water.

This bull is ready to rumble...

The male sea lions are always battling for the best habitat. Keep an eye on that big bull, because this is his territory and he's going to defend it. The battles between bulls can be extreme—there is blood, flesh is torn, sometimes there is death. Every bull wants oceanfront real estate. The strongest bull, with the best habitat, attracts the most females. He reproduces with them, thus passing on his strong genes to the next generation.

This bull isn't too happy about having us on his property. We'll give him some space.

Pups love being close to each other.

Pups are fun!

    Hopefully, the pups in this
group will be friendlier. There's plenty of activity here, with pups
playing around in little pools. It's in these shallows that the animals
practice their swimming skills. When it's time for them to venture
out on their own, they have all the skills they need to survive. But
at this age the pups are most vulnerable.

    These pups just love being close to each other. They love con-
tact. They love to lic on each other and be close. Sometimes you
can see these animals pile up on each other, huge piles of sea lions.

Can you spot all the sea lions in this picture?

Plaza Sur is surrounded by an incredible underwater habitat.

The beautiful water surrounding Plaza Sur is as densely populated with life as the land. This is a part of the Galápagos that Darwin never had a chance to witness. And even here, underwater, his principles are being acted out. This wonderland is in constant flux, and animals must adapt in order to survive.

Now, I know you're supposed to let sleeping sharks lie, but look at this guy. For years, scientists believed that the only way sharks could breathe was by moving, so that water would go in their mouth and through their gills. But here are sharks that are breathing and they're not moving. There have been so many sightings of groups like this, lying motionless, that new theories have to be considered. Are these sharks resting? Is this a shark social gathering? A prelude to mating? The jury is still out in scientific circles.

Next, something you'd never expect to see in the tropics.

LOOK AT THIS!

Like most all other fish, sharks (with a few exceptions), get oxygen into their blood in their gills. Most sharks swim with their mouth open, so that water can flow over the gills. As the water passes over the gills, the blood in the gills takes up oxygen and leaves the waste product of carbon dioxide. The carbon dioxide is then transported away with the outgoing water leaving the gills.

Certain species (like some found in the Galápagos) don't have to swim to breathe. Instead, they keep a steady stream of water over the gills by pumping with their mouths. Many bottom-dwelling species take in water through a spiracle, which is actually a hole behind the eye. They pump the water out through the gills, which also prevents bottom sediments from being inhaled.

Bony fishes have gills that are covered by a lid, called an operculum, but cartilaginous fishes (sharks and rays) don't have these lids. Instead, they have a series of gill slits (one for each gill arch, altogether five to seven) out of which the water flows. Fossil remains show that some pre-historic sharks had as many as ten pairs of gill arches. The more gill arches a fish has, the more primitive it is thought to be. Throughout the millions of years that fish have existed, evolution has led to fewer and fewer gill arches. Sharks that have six or seven gill arches (e.g. frilled sharks, cow sharks) are therefore believed to be more primitive than those with five gill arches.

The island of Mariella.

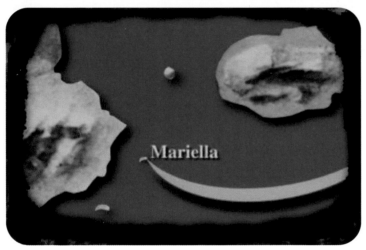

Mariella

We've traveled 65 miles to the island of Mariella. I'm not sure if Darwin stopped here on his voyage in 1835, but he should have. We're 6,000 miles from Antarctica, but this island is home to penguins.

Like other penguins, the Galápagos penguin is not much of a walker. He hops from one place to the next, and on land these birds are not what you'd call graceful. But in the water, they're like their own Bolshoi ballet.

Yup. Penguins in the tropics.

They're not the most graceful things on two legs...

Penguins spend a lot of time preening, grooming their feathers. This is a very important behavior for these animals. The water around these islands is fed by some extremely cold currents, the Humboldt and the Cromwell currents. That cold water provides these creatures with the food they need, sardines and mullet. But they really have to be careful with regard to their body temperature. They can easily suffer from hypothermia. Their only defense is a half-inch-thick layer of very dense feathers. And they continually preen the feathers to make sure they're compact and well lubricated. That provides a barrier between the icy water and their warm flesh.

Many scientists believe that the Galápagos penguins are a cross between the Humboldt and the Magellan penguins. Their ancestors made their way here millions of years ago from the southern tip of South America. As with many of the amazing creatures living in the Galápagos, they were isolated and over time evolved into a new species, no longer kin to the penguins from South America.

The Galápagos penguins are a species unique to this environment.

Penguins are excellent parents. They spend nearly a year raising their babies, investing so much energy that the offspring can weigh more than the parents!

Penguin parents are good providers.

The babies get big because they do nothing but sit, eat, and grow. Their parents are swimming, gathering up tons of sardines and mullet, which they swallow and bring back in their stomachs. Then the parents regurgitate the fish as a sort of mush and feed it to their babies. That's very cool, but I'm glad a penguin isn't my mother.

Penguins aren't the only animals on little Mariella Island. We've got blue-footed boobies. We've got flightless cormorants. We've got Sally Lightfoot crabs. And we just saw an octopus come out of the water, chasing a Sally Lightfoot crab. He didn't get it, but it was amazing.

Octopus

I love those boobies with blue feet.

Look at this baby tortoise.

I'm on Santa Cruz Island, at a structure that's kind of like a green-house—not for growing flowers, but for very special creatures, Galápagos tortoises. It's part of the national park system, connected with the Darwin Center, and the naturalists here are raising baby tortoises.

For millions of years, these animals flourished in the Galápagos Islands. But when human beings arrived, things changed very quickly, because ships passing through the area would stop here to stock up on tortoise. Sailors could keep these animals alive on ships for up to a year without food or water, and have access to fresh meat, and fat to fire up an oil lamp, and even water collected in this creature's bladder. Hunting nearly wiped out the tortoises. In four centuries, their numbers were reduced from about two hundred thousand to less than thirteen thousand. Two types actually became extinct because of the behavior of human beings.

Here's a tortoise I want to show you, a beautiful tortoise, and I'll share a banana with him. He's a Cerro Azul, or Blue Hill, tortoise. If you look at the shell of this individual, you'll notice that it's missing some of its scutes. This creature was injured in 1998, when a volcano erupted. Lava flowed from Cerro Azul to Sierra Negra, and unfortunately this turtle was in the way and was burned. Some of the tortoises were transported to safety by helicopter. But this individual, which weighs hundreds of pounds, was hand carried by some very dedicated and concerned park rangers. He was reha-

This is a Blue Hill tortoise...

bilitated, and now he's a part of the very important breeding program here. He's also an ambassador for this place, sharing the important natural history of these very wonderful turtles.

There's another kind of tortoise that looks like it's been run over by a steamroller, but it's supposed to look like that. It's an extraordinary animal—a Cinco Cerros, or Five Hills, tortoise that has evolved a very flat back, while others have a round shell. So, what does this mean? Are we seeing Darwin's theories come to life? Are we seeing some part of the adaptive process? Is this an isolated phenomenon or the start of a new species? The answer to that will probably come in about a million years.

Look at that skin...

This park is an important place for turtles to mate.

Yikes! I better stand back!

When we think of tortoises, we think of quiet animals. But these animals aren't quiet during the breeding season. When they mate, the males roar and utter a groaning sound. Reproduction is the goal at this breeding center within the Galápagos National Park, where naturalists hope to secure the future not only of Cinco Cerro tortoises but of other Galápagos tortoises as well.

These creatures may live a hundred years or more. No one really knows their actual life span. It's quite possible that there is a tortoise on one of the Galápagos Islands that's been hanging around since the days of Darwin.

This fellow's an herbivore, but he's looking at me like I'm the biggest banana he ever saw. Time to go.

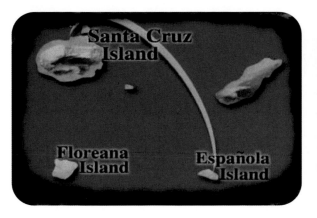

Here's a colony of boobies.

It has taken us ten hours to sail from Santa Cruz to Española, the most southern of the Galápagos Islands. Some excellent stuff is happening here. We've got a small colony of masked boobies, birds with some very interesting, complex behavior.

The masked booby is named for the featherless area of brown skin around its bill. The female masked booby lays two eggs, but the parents will raise only one offspring. One of those eggs hatches first, perhaps a week before the other egg. Then, when the second egg hatches, the first hatchling pushes the second hatchling outside the boundary of the nest site, sort of an invisible circle around the nest.

See the mask?

Booby babies are fuzzy at first.

Checking out a booby nest.

The parents ignore the battle as that little hatchling is pushed out. And even though the second hatchling is only a neck length away from its parents, they ignore it as it bakes in the hot sun and starves to death. The winning hatchling survives and is cared for by the parents. This behavior, in which one offspring kills the other for 100 percent of the parents' attention, is called "obligate siblicide" or the "Cain and Abel" effect.

Española is a beautiful island, one of the oldest islands in this archipelago, almost 3 million years in age. It's home to a splendid lizard, a gorgeous marine iguana. To find it, just look where you're standing because

These marine iguanas are gorgeous.

Spiny backs help protect these lizards.

they're all around. Look at the colors—they're like lizards wrapped in rainbows, and the individuals all have different colorations. This one has a turquoise blue stripe going down his spine.

These iguanas bob their heads to communicate with each other, to warn other lizards out of their territory. Scientists think the different colors also have something to do with competition between individual lizards. The wildlife is packed very tightly in this island, and these iguanas are smaller than those on some of the other islands. They compete with each other with color rather than size. If you're an iguana, the prettier you are and the more spectacular your color, the better chance you have of getting a mate. Your color advertises your health and fitness.

This female iguana digs a nest and will defend it fiercely.

This female iguana is working hard to excavate a nest. She'll dig a half a meter or more into the earth, ripping away plant roots and pulling out stones and soil. But she must also defend her territory from other females, who may dig up and destroy her eggs and then claim the nest for their own.

A female stands guard when another female comes near her nest. She opens her mouth and bobs her head to say, "Get out of here. Get out of my nest!" And after she drives off her competitor, she returns to the nest for a little victory dance, a little victory digging, and eventually some victory egg laying.

Our next destination is Isla Isabela. It is the largest of the Galápagos Islands, and it's home to some equally large creatures.

The Isla Isabela iguanas are huge!

Not only is Isabela the largest of the islands, but it's still growing. Five central volcanoes form the spine of the island, and they're still active.

The marine iguanas here have adapted to the spaciousness of the island. They're huge. I feel like I'm in a 1950s Japanese horror movie.

Five volcanoes are still active.

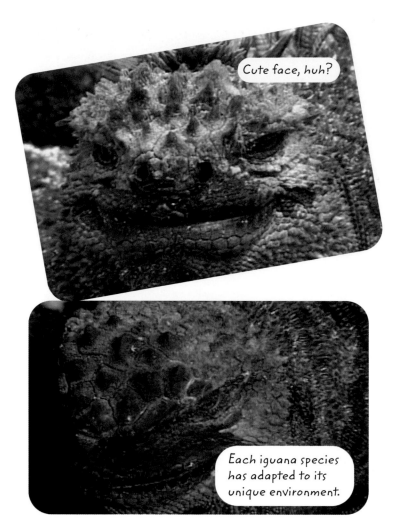

Cute face, huh?

Each iguana species has adapted to its unique environment.

As we come face to face with the various types of iguanas in the Galápagos, we're seeing Darwin's theories come to life. This animal illustrates a theory known as adaptive radiation. This is when a species adapts to survive in a very specific environment. Here each island hosts a new and different subspecies, shaped by its environment. Adaptations help these animals survive, and the survivors breed and pass on their adaptations to their offspring.

Look at this guy—he's a serious male. He's showing his orna-mentation and his strength. Not only does he have a great array of spines going down his body, but he's so old that they're actually folding over each other. Those triangular scales on his head come in handy for spar-ring head to head with other male iguanas, as they wrestle back and forth over access to a

This male is a serious dude...

good plot of rock where all the girls are going to be hanging out. This is the look of a creature that's fit to survive, and to a female iguana he's one very handsome fellow.

This land iguana is a beauty.

Check out this profile.

So far, I've only shown you marine iguanas, but here, finally, is a Galápagos land iguana. Look at its colors. The top is coppery, while the bottom and the head are a beautiful yellow and the eyes are red. This individual is a male, with raised spines and domelike bumps on his head. As you can see, these lizards are solid muscle. They use the muscles in their arms and legs to climb up trees in search of fruit and food. Females use the powerful muscles in their legs and those powerful claws to rip apart the earth to lay their eggs.

Land iguanas like this have a very long life span. Marine iguanas live to about thirty years, but these creatures can live about sixty years. If Darwin were alive today, he'd be amazed at some of

These iguanas are pure muscle.

Strong arms and legs enable these guys to climb.

the adaptations of these iguanas. Scientists believe that the land iguanas of Isabela have evolved to such an extent that they're well under way to becoming their own species.

Here in the Galápagos we get a rare window into the world of these animals. We can just sit here while a few feet away this creature goes about its business with not a care in the world. The animals here have evolved in many ways that promote their survival, but one behavior they do not possess is a fear of being hunted. That's because animals have been allowed to evolve for millions of years on these islands without predators.

East of Isabela, beyond Santa Cruz, is an island where something special is happening.

Is it a marine animal...?

...Or a land animal?

Look at this lizard. It is no ordinary reptile. This iguana is a hybrid, the product of a mating between a marine and a land iguana.

Ten million years ago, the ancestors of land and marine iguanas arrived in these islands.

Then some of their descendants split into one group that ate the algae in the ocean—the marine iguanas. And the other group took refuge on land and ate cactus and other plants. Now there's this fellow, part marine and part land.

How do we know it's a hybrid? The first thing you notice is the color—it's very black, just like the marine iguanas. You don't see the yellow that you would find on a land iguana, but you do see some whitish pigment, which is often seen around the neck

Whitish pigment and a flat muzzle are two tips that this is a hybrid.

of the land iguanas. Here it's broken up by the black.

Next, notice that the muzzle on this beast is very flat and rounded. That's something you'd see in marine iguanas, which need a flat muzzle to graze on seaweed.

This is something of a new species.

This mixing of two species is very new. This has just happened in the last few years, and we really don't know where it's going to go. As a naturalist, I find it exciting to come face-to-face with what might be a new creature. We're witnessing the words of Darwin coming to life. Maybe this is the start of a new species, with its own characteristics for survival. Or maybe it's an experiment that ends here. To get the real answer, just stick around for a couple of thousand years.

Our Galápagos adventure has been such a dramatic series of encounters that I think it deserves a big ending. We're back on the majestic island of Isabela to wrap up our journey at Sierra Negra, the second largest caldera, or volcanic crater, in the world. At some points it's 5.5 miles across. A million years ago, it was violent. Lava bubbled up from the earth and fried everything in its path. But in the end, out of that violence came life. The lava cooled and formed a substrate, a surface for life forms to grow on. First came the plants, and then came the animals.

Out there is a caldera.

Millions of years ago this baby was spitting out hot lava night and day.

The Galápagos Islands are an extraordinary place. This living laboratory of evolution has drawn scientists for years and years—first Darwin and then others. They come to better understand our world and the amazing process of evolution. But I think it's important for us to remember that, although many of the creatures that live here are hardy in nature, overall this is a very sensitive place. What we do here can have an impact, and we might as well make a positive one.

Until we meet again, I look forward to our next wildlife experience.

Glossary

caldera the crater left by a volcano

cartilaginous composed of or related to cartilage

cornucopia a large amount

crustacean a type of aquatic animal such as a shrimp, crab, or lobster

evolution Darwin's theory to explain how species adapt and change
over time

extinct when no more members of a species are alive

flux movement or change

habitat a place where animals and plants live naturally together

herbivore an animal that eats plants

hybrid the offspring of two different kinds of animals

hypothermia subnormal temperature of the body

metabolism processes in the body necessary for life, such as getting energy
from food

naturalist a student of natural history such as a field biologist

obligate siblicide when one baby animal kills its sibling to get all of its
parents' attention

operculum the covering of a fish's gills

predators animals that kill and eat other animals

preening cleaning and grooming

rain forest a tropical forest that receives a lot of rain

rehabilitated healed, restored to health

reptiles cold-blooded, usually egg-laying animals such as snakes or lizards

scutes bony plates or scales, such as on a turtle's shell

spiracle a breathing hole

substrate the surface of the earth that animals live on

tropics places close to the equator

Index